To

_____

From

_____

Date

_____

Because You Care

CECIL MURPHEY
TWILA BELK

Photography by BETTY FLETCHER

HARVEST HOUSE PUBLISHERS

EUGENE, OREGON

Because You Care

Text Copyright © 2012 by Cecil Murphey and Twila Belk
Artwork Copyright © 2012 by Betty Fletcher

Published by Harvest House Publishers
Eugene, Oregon 97402
www.harvesthousepublishers.com

ISBN 978-0-7369-4328-4

Cecil Murphey and Twila Belk are represented by Deidre Knight, The Knight Agency; 570 East Avenue, Madison, GA 30650; Phone 404-538-2030; Fax 706-752-1158; Deidre.knight@knightagency.net

Design and production by Koechel Peterson and Associates, Inc., Minneapolis, Minnesota

Special thanks to Gail Smith for her insightful help with this book.

All Scripture quotations are from the *Holy Bible,* New Living Translation, copyright © 1996, 2004. Used by permission of Tyndale House Publishers, Inc., Wheaton, IL 60189 USA. All rights reserved.

Printed in China

12 13 14 15 16 17 18 / FC / 10 9 8 7 6 5 4 3 2 1

CONTENTS

This Is Who You Are

From Cec and Twila

Others may call you brave. They'll use words like *noble* or *sacrificial*. They'll admire and applaud you because you've offered your life to make yourself available to someone who needs a long-term caregiver.

"I couldn't do what you're doing for him," a friend says.

You listen to the words your friend speaks, and you like hearing the compliments. Yet as you listen and smile, you don't see yourself as exceptional. You're doing the right thing for someone you love, and that gives you peace. You also know the reason you've devoted your energies to another person.

You can express that reason in a single sentence: "I do it because I care." You might say it's because you love the person, or you may do it because of a strong sense of commitment to God and to your loved one. Regardless of how you express yourself, you're determined to give yourself as fully as you can.

Some days you may not feel like loving anyone. You get tired, lose your temper, or think of the things you didn't accomplish. During the worst times, you wish the situation would change. And in those dark moments, you've probably prayed, *Dear Lord, please take this burden from me.*

> Caring for your loved one wasn't part of your dream, but this is the life you have.

The situation probably won't change for a long time—perhaps years. It's not the kind of life you would have imagined. You probably envisioned living out your years in blissful peace. Caring for your loved one wasn't part of your dream, but this is the life you have. Despite the moments of sadness, perhaps even regret, your answer remains the same: "I care."

❈ ❈ ❈ ❈ ❈ ❈ ❈ ❈ ❈

Both of us are long-term caregivers, although our situations are different. Twila's husband, Steve, suffers from a deteriorating illness. There are no medications and no cures. He also has bipolar disorder which sometimes exacerbates his condition. Twila will care for Steve as long as she is able. She knows a day will come when she won't be able to lift him and give him the tender attention he needs. When she peers into the future, sometimes she sheds a few tears. But this is her life now. It's her divinely given role.

When Cecil ("Cec") and Shirley married, they accepted the reality that Shirley wasn't physically strong. In their more than fifty years together, many of her days have been spent in pain. Her disabilities began in childhood with a rheumatic heart condition. She then experienced a serious automobile accident in her twenties, breast cancer in her sixties, and now faces heart disease.

From the beginning of their marriage, Cec was aware that he would likely survive her and become her caregiver as they aged together. "I love her," he says. "I promised God I'd stand with her 'in sickness and in health.'"

Neither Cec nor Twila knows what lies ahead for them, but both share the deep inner peace that God has made them long-term caregivers. Like others, this isn't what they would have chosen, but this is the reality they face each day.

The First Words

From Twila

"You'll need to see a specialist," Dr. Wright said.

He spoke the words I didn't want to hear. A specialist meant Steve's condition was serious.

"Amyotrophic lateral sclerosis," the physician said as the final of three possible diagnoses.

"You mean Lou Gehrig's disease?" I asked. Because I had once been a medical transcriptionist, I knew the language.

I stared at the doctor, but my thoughts raced to the memory of a man in our church who had died of Lou Gehrig's disease. Don had once been vibrant, but the disease progressed rapidly. Within a year, he had been unable to do the simplest tasks. I wanted to ask if that was the way it would be with Steve.

Before I asked, Dr. Wright repeated, "You'll need to see a specialist."

With that second statement, my life changed in every way because I took on a new label in life. I cared for someone who was seriously ill.

The most difficult fact for me to absorb—and I wasn't able to do that for several days—was the third statement that remains sealed inside my heart: "There will be no recovery."

The specialist's diagnosis wasn't ALS but a rare muscle disease with many common characteristics. They call it "inclusion body myositis."

But worse than the disease were the two words I had to face and didn't want to admit: *No recovery.*

Steve's condition will grow steadily worse.

No treatment will slow down the progress.

We had started to travel on an expressway without interchanges and would continue until we reached the end of that road called "Together."

I took on a new label in life...I cared for someone who was seriously ill.

❁ ❁ ❁ ❁ ❁ ❁ ❁ ❁ ❁

From Cec

During our dating days, Shirley didn't try to minimize her poor health or make it sound worse. I was aware of it and accepted it.

The first words to awaken me came at our wedding when Pastor Olson asked me to pledge myself to her "in sickness and in health until death do us part."

At age twenty-two, I wasn't ready to begin the role of caregiver, and Shirley was fairly healthy during that period. Although any kind of permanent disability seemed like something too far into the future to comprehend, I sensed what lay ahead for both of us. I didn't have full comprehension, of course, only a vague assurance that the good years we'd share would more than compensate for what lay ahead.

In a way, it's strange that Shirley and I had fallen in love with each other. I call myself boringly healthy and rarely feel pain; I love a woman who has known few days without pain.

That's not a complaint. I'm grateful for every day we have together.

Each morning when I awaken, I glance at Shirley, who is usually still asleep. *Thank you, God,* I whisper, *that we have at least one more day together.*

Even as I say those words, I know that eventually we will face our final moments with each other.

That's when I expect to say, *Thank you, God, for the days we were able to share.*

Life Will Never Be the Same

From Rose

My father had always been a robust man who could effortlessly pick up a fifty-pound bag of dog food. Now he struggles to press a key on his computer. What formerly were simple and ordinary tasks for him have become major and often unattainable. He's dependent on me for almost everything.

I miss my dad of days past and wish his health hadn't deteriorated. I often reminisce about the long walks during my childhood or the times we worked in the garden after he first came to live with us. Sometimes tears form in my eyes when I tell my husband, "It isn't easy. Caring for Dad takes a lot of my time and most of my energy."

One day I had lunch with Wilma, a member of my Sunday school class. When she asked about Dad, I said, "I love him, but he's—well, difficult at times." She didn't say anything. I related several stories of the extra work he caused and how tired I felt some nights.

"I'm sorry," she said. "So sorry for all—"

"This probably sounds strange," I said, "after all I've just said. And it's true, but…but—"

She looked quizzically at me.

"But it's an honor to be able to help him through this. I'm thankful for the opportunity to take care of him."

> I don't think I would have understood words like *compassion* and *tenderness* if it hadn't been for him.

As we talked, I blurted out, "Because of his living with us, I've opened up more to God and learned many invaluable lessons about life. I don't think I would have understood words like *compassion* and *tenderness* if it hadn't been for him."

"That's an amazing insight," Wilma said.

I nodded because it was the first time I had ever spoken those words. Yet they were true. "I've become a different person—a better person—because of giving much of my life and energy to care for my father."

"It can't be easy caring for someone else, and obviously the strain brings out the worst in you—"

"But it has also brought out the best in me."

I closed my eyes and silently thanked God. In the midst of complaining about Dad, I also realized I had become a better, stronger person.

After I left Wilma, I thought, *It's natural to grieve the loss of what was and become stuck in the past.* I often have to remind myself that my life will never be the way it once was.

I wish Dad were healthy once again, but I'm determined to live life as it is now. I want to move forward and discover purpose in each new day.

Most long-term caregivers learn that life won't ever be the way it was before their loved ones became ill. It's a truth they face daily.

Life will never be the same.
I will never be the same,
but I will continue to grow
and to value life.

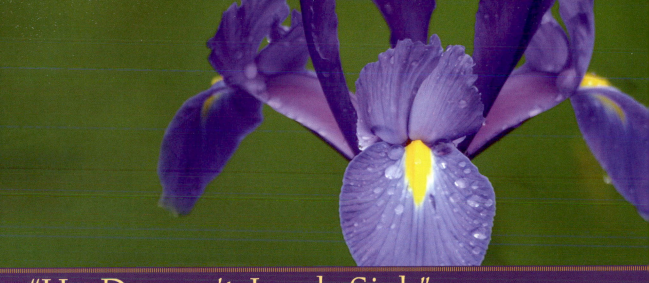

"He Doesn't Look Sick"

From Twila

"Steve doesn't look sick," my friend said. "I expected him to, you know—"

"It's a progressive disease and—"

"But that's the way it is with everybody," he said and shrugged. "We're all progressing toward the end. Everybody is terminal. We all die eventually, and then we go to be with Jesus."

"But his muscles atrophy—" I tried to explain, but I don't think he heard the words. His harsh tone made it clear that he really wasn't interested in Steve.

The conversation left me bewildered. It wasn't the first time, and I'm sure it won't be the last that I didn't know how to react to insensitive remarks. Just because my husband doesn't look disabled doesn't mean he hasn't fallen multiple times or that he doesn't struggle when he climbs the stairs.

Most people assume that seriously ill people look wan, haggard, and listless, carry oxygen around with them, or sit in wheelchairs. Some diseases attack from within, and it takes a long time before it shows outwardly. Even though Steve looks healthy, his disease is incurable and crippling.

When people ask Steve how he feels, he usually says, "I'm doing all right."

I know differently because I live with him. One day he dropped a jar of spaghetti sauce in the grocery store. I pushed the cart into another aisle while store personnel cleaned up the splattered mess. I was embarrassed by the situation and embarrassed for my husband. *He doesn't look sick,* I thought, *so people have no idea that he dropped the jar because he has no strength to grip it.* For days I felt guilty for running away.

Another time, the crowd at our son's basketball game gasped when my husband stepped off the bleachers and fell to the floor. He didn't have enough quadricep strength to hold up. My heart hurt for him, yet I didn't know what to do other than help him up and say, "Honey, are you okay?"

> Do not depend on your own understanding.

A few weeks later, Steve fell on the minigolf course and tried to laugh it off by saying he needed to look before he stepped into a hole. He had the rest of the group laughing.

I didn't laugh; I turned away because I felt like crying.

One day, as I cried out to God for answers and understanding, I read Proverbs 3:5-6: "Trust in the LORD with all your heart; do not depend on your own understanding. Seek his will in all you do, and he will show you which path to take."

I'd read those verses many times, but that day I had an insightful moment. The words "Do not depend on your own understanding" became real to me. I sensed God had whispered that I didn't have to know everything—that I wasn't *supposed* to know everything. I needed only to trust.

Those simple, often-quoted words from Proverbs gave me great comfort. I frequently encounter things I don't understand about Steve's progressive illness. I don't comprehend why God doesn't answer my prayers for my husband to get better. Why is there no medication or treatment for his disease?

Most of the time, I'm able to push away those thoughts, but when I can't, I remind myself of those wise words from Proverbs. My responsibility is to care for the person I love most. If I acknowledge God's love for Steve and for me, he'll lead me to do what's right and what's best for my husband. I've received great comfort from repeating those simple words.

Caring for someone I love isn't always easy, but I cope day by day. I know that the journey ahead will be even more difficult as his disease advances. I don't have a how-to manual to teach me how to protect Steve from insensitive people.

Like many others, I still struggle to respond to those who don't grasp the seriousness of our situation, but I have peace knowing that I don't have to explain. It hurts *me* when I hear thoughtless or uninformed remarks. But as I trust God for guidance and for strength, I find peace. Despite my inadequacy in the role of caregiver, I do the best I can.

That's enough, isn't it? As one of my friends says, "All you can do is all you can do." To others, he doesn't look sick, and I can't always protect him when he drops something or can't walk normally down the steps. I can care and I do.

I also remind myself of those powerful words from Proverbs, and each day I learn to live those words a little more.

"Do not depend on your own understanding."
— God

Reading the Eyes

From Cec

I hugged Shirley this morning and asked, "How are you?"

"All right."

That's her common response because she doesn't indulge in self-pity, and she doesn't want me to feel sorry for her. I stepped back, held her by the shoulders, and stared at her.

Her eyes were clear. "I believe you," I said and embraced her again.

Each morning when I hold her for our first daily hug, I stare into her blue eyes. Sometimes I don't have to ask how she feels because I can see the pain. Perhaps the ability to read her eyes comes from our years of living together and being aware of her many physical problems.

Reading her eyes is my way of getting an accurate report from her. She's the most important person in my life, and I truly want to know how she feels.

"The eyes can't lie." I once used those words to chide Shirley when she said she felt fine. She wasn't fine; she hurt, and I could see it clearly.

Her words weren't an intentional lie, and she said, "I get tired of being fussed over."

That's a big difference between us. I often joke that if I have a headache, I want everyone's sympathy. Maybe that's because I haven't been seriously ill or gone through any lingering disease. Pain is Shirley's frequent companion, and she doesn't want me or anyone else to focus on how bad she feels.

Because I love her, I naturally focus on her suffering and pray faithfully for her. Each day as I "read" her eyes, I yearn for a sign that she's better. Some days she is; some days she's worse.

❧ ❧ ❧ ❧ ❧ ❧ ❧ ❧ ❧

Those of us who love the seriously ill have our ways of judging their day-by-day health. Some caregivers watch the loved one when he walks. One woman referred to the "hurt lines" in her

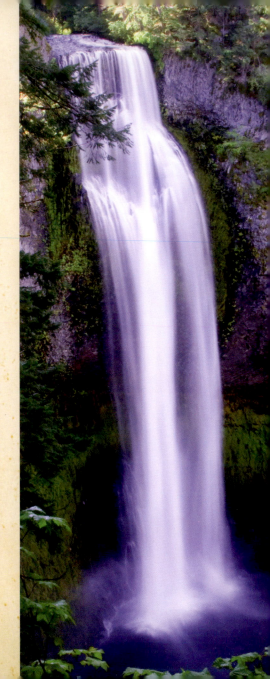

20

husband's face. Another woman said, "As soon as he speaks, his voice tells me how he feels."

How we read our loved one's condition isn't nearly as important as our need for the opportunity to express our love and affirm our ongoing commitment.

The other day I thought, *If I don't ask about her health or look into her eyes, how would she feel? Would I come across as indifferent? Not caring? Not loving?* Possibly. I wouldn't want that. I want her to know of my concern.

One man told me his wife seldom said anything to him to express care. For several years he silently worried that she might leave him or put him in a nursing home before he needed to be in one.

I've decided to stare into Shirley's blue eyes every morning because that's where I'll discover how she feels. I'll ask the same question because it's the best way for me to express my love.

I'm glad we can learn to read our loved ones. We don't feel their pain or suffer as they do, but someone said we must suffer silently. Our pain isn't physical, but it still hurts.

Dear loving God, remind both of us of your presence. We don't understand why life is the way it is, but we've committed ourselves to cherish each other in times of robust health and just as much in times of long-term sickness.

The Worst Words

From Twila

One day his doctor spoke the words we weren't able to say aloud: "He won't get any better."

The doctor didn't say he'll be an invalid or that he'll survive for only a year. Without intending to do so, however, he has smashed our hopes. He has trampled on any illusions we've cherished for our loved one to improve.

He won't get better.

That means he'll only get worse.

We want to focus on our loved ones recovering, improving, or receiving enough medicine to eliminate the intense suffering. We look for cures and expect the innovations and research to produce wonders. Miracle drugs. Total relief.

"If they can make nuclear bombs, why can't they find a cure?" someone asks. In our painful despair, we may cry out with similar statements. We're really saying, "I love him. I don't want to lose him."

But I will lose him.

He won't get better.

"It's all downhill," one friend said after she heard the prognosis for her sister. After that, she became aware of the slightest change in her sister's body. She watched even more closely. "She won't get any better," my friend said for the fourth time that morning.

Except for some divine miracle or breakthrough medical treatment, nothing will change that diagnosis. Each day, like my friend, I can only watch as my loved one slowly diminishes.

Sometimes I think Steve's body has deteriorated a lot during the past year.

Six months ago he was able to go up and down a flight of stairs. Today, he tries to hide the grimace he makes as he takes each step.

I've heard the worst words.

Now I'm learning to live with them.

I've heard the worst words. Now I'm learning to live with them.

Dear God, you invented love, and you
taught us to love. I didn't realize how
much love could hurt. As I become
aware of his increased suffering,
I want it taken away. It won't go away,
so please make me strong enough to
cope with my own suffering.

Facing Guilt

From Cec

"Don't go to bed feeling guilty," my friend Eleanor said. She had been caring for her mother for two years.

No matter how hard Eleanor tried or how caring she was, she seemed to feel a residual guilt for leaving things undone. Several times she talked to my wife and me about never having enough hours in the day, feeling overwhelmed by her tasks, and knowing there would always be things she couldn't accomplish.

"I do my best for Mama, but I have a husband and other obligations," Eleanor said while sitting in our living room. "It was a little easier after we moved Mama into what used to be our daughter's room." Even so, for a long time Eleanor continued to feel guilty and inefficient at the end of the day. One day she learned to deal with those feelings and receive the rest she desperately needed. Eleanor explained, "Each night I repeat the words, 'I refuse to feel guilty anymore,' before I can get to sleep. Even then I often have to add, 'I did the best I could today.'"

Some people should feel guilty because they are neglectful, insensitive, or unaware of their failures. Eleanor doesn't have anything to say to them, but from her own experience, she can talk to those of us who live with *undeserved* guilt.

There are no magic answers, but here's one thing Eleanor passed on to me. She explained, "When I go to bed, I ask myself: *Have I done what I could for Mama?* A few times I could have done more and didn't. In those instances, I ask God to forgive me for failing. Then I say to myself: *I forgive you for not being perfect. I forgive you for doing less than you could.*"

After that Eleanor asks God to help her become more sensitive to her mother's needs. She told me, "I want to be able to drift into a peaceful sleep thinking, *I did my best today. Imperfect, yes, but it was my best.*"

At times she has to repeat the words and remind herself that she has no supernatural powers, and then she whispers, "I offer what I have to give."

When I give what I have,
God reminds me that it is enough.

"Was It Something I Did?"

Lynda's Story

I stared into my son's dark brown eyes and could see that he was deeply troubled. He mentioned that his friends were healthy and then went on to ask, "Why am I sick while my friends aren't?" He paused, and his lips trembled before he added, "Was it something I did?"

My immediate reaction was to say, "Certainly not," and try to assure him that it wasn't. Instead, I gently kissed his cheek and said, "I don't know why you're sick. Nobody knows why some children become ill and others don't. But I know God loves you, and I love you."

I didn't sense that was the right answer, so I asked, "What makes you feel it's your fault?"

27

He blinked several times, and his eyes filled with tears. "I've done bad things." Before I could ask, he told me about lying to me once. Another time he cheated on a test at school. For three or four minutes, he confessed all the wrongdoings he could remember.

"I'm glad you told me," I said. "God has forgiven you, and I hope you feel better now."

"A little."

"God loves you very much," I said. "We all do bad things at times, but God didn't make you sick because of anything you did."

I thought of trying to give him a fuller explanation, but he smiled and closed his eyes. That seemed to be enough.

You [God] will keep in perfect peace all who trust in you…

— Isaiah 26:3

I realize that sometimes there are reasons children become sick or get injured, such as when a child foolishly drinks a harmful substance or plays with a dangerous tool. But most of the time, we don't have the answer.

Two days ago I spoke with a father and mother who struggled with the same question of divine retribution. "Is God punishing our daughter because of something I did or we did?" the husband asked.

"We've confessed everything we can think of and asked for forgiveness," the wife said.

"We've both gone over and over our shortcomings, failures, and sins—"

"Because you think that God is getting even with you by punishing your daughter?" I asked.

He nodded and said softly, "Yes."

"I don't know the answer," I told them, "but I do know God isn't out to punish you for every little thing you do wrong."

"But it's so hard to understand," she said.

"God doesn't promise you'll be able to understand why," I said, "but he does promise his presence."

"My thoughts are nothing like your thoughts," says the LORD. "And my ways are far beyond anything you could imagine. For just as the heavens are higher than the earth, so my ways are higher than your ways and my thoughts higher than your thoughts."

— ISAIAH 55:8-9

Protecting Him

From Twila

"He has only so much muscle strength to use," the neurologist at Mayo Clinic said. "Once the strength is gone, it's gone forever."

The doctor clearly told me that muscle-exerting activities would further break down Steve's muscles rather than build them up.

My husband denied hearing that message. I don't know the reason for his refusal to hear, but I wonder if it's because he's afraid to acknowledge the reality. By not hearing the words he doesn't have to grapple with the diagnosis.

That explanation—true or not—helps me understand his attitude when I try to do things for him. "I'm not an invalid," he says. So I pull back and allow him to do for himself what he can.

As the days pass, I watch the progressive deterioration of the strong man I married. I observe his thinning legs and the lack of muscle mass in his arms. I look away when he struggles to hold his silverware, button his shirt, or open a door.

He tries to do his own vehicle repairs and insists he can still carry bags of groceries from the car and boxes of books to the post office. He's determined to continue playing catch with our thirteen-year-old son and pitches him baseballs for batting practice even though he can't properly grip the ball.

As the one responsible for his care, I'm concerned that he's overdoing it, but I have to watch in silence.

> The mother in me wants to protect him; the wife in me wants to extend his longevity.

The mother in me wants to protect him; the wife in me wants to extend his longevity. The caregiver in me selfishly doesn't want him to get hurt because I know it means more work for me.

Why is this so difficult? How do I handle this? Should I try to control his mobility and stop him from physical exertion? Or do I honor his manhood by allowing him to do whatever he wants? I can't trust that he'll know when to stop, so how much do I interfere?

I try not to take over even though I could fasten all his buttons while he struggles with the first one. He tries so hard to prove to me—and perhaps to himself—that he's not getting weaker. It's not easy for me to be the quiet-but-supportive caregiver. Sometimes I promise God that I won't interfere. Before long, however, I'm back into the protective mode again. I struggle with guilt for doing too much or feel ashamed for doing too little.

What would it be like if I were in his position? How would I feel if I were stripped of my independence because of physical illness? Maybe I'd be just like him. Maybe I would resent anyone helping me.

Daily I seek an answer—*the* answer—to the situation. If I were only a wife or merely his caregiver, perhaps I could find a simple solution. But I'm both and I love him.

His stubbornness upsets me, and sometimes I lose my temper. "Why don't you do what I say?" I want to yell. I stop myself, but I think he knows how I feel.

Sometimes I want to scream, "It's difficult to care for a loved one who will never get better." But again, I don't say those words aloud. Sometimes I wish the medical staff had given me an instruction book about the things I need to do for him. But his illness didn't come with guidelines, and so I cope by praying much and loving more fully.

Lord, I wrestle with how to help my loved
one and do what's best for him. I can't help it
because I want to protect him. I don't want him
to think I treat him as if he's an invalid. Give me
the discernment to know how to intervene
when he tries to do too much.

Someone Who Understands

From Hannah

"It isn't supposed to be this way." I pounded the table in anger. "I had dreams for my child. She was supposed to grow up healthy and take care of me when I get old."

Jackie nodded in understanding and gently covered my hand with her own. "I used to think that way. I was devastated and confused about my son's situation, just as you are with Emma's, and—"

"I envisioned my baby girl playing with her siblings and friends. I dreamed of the long shopping trips we'd take and the parties we'd plan together." I stopped to wipe the tears from my eyes. "I wanted her to go to college and get into a profession that would change lives." Despite my efforts, tears streaked my face. "Now—"

"And then the unexpected happened."

Unable to speak, I nodded.

"Things didn't go as I had planned either. I wondered how I'd ever be able to accept the fact that Joey wouldn't be like other kids and that my life was no longer mine to control," Jackie said, sipping her hot tea and sitting quietly for a few seconds as her memories returned. "Sometimes I would scream at God, 'How could you let this happen?'"

"*You?* You did that?" I replied. Jackie was such a fine Christian and always seemed tranquil. "I've screamed at God, but I didn't think you—"

"If we hurt badly enough, we scream," she said softly. "And yes, I blamed God—just as you do—at least I did at first."

I burst into tears, and Jackie wisely let me cry.

When I looked up at her, I asked, "How did you get to the point of acceptance?"

"After I got tired of blaming God, my doctors, and myself and hating the world in general, I cried out to God...for a very, very long time. People I didn't even know prayed for me," she continued as she reached out to touch my hand again, "just as I have been praying for you."

I wondered if I could ever have that peaceful, gentle spirit like Jackie had.

As if she could read my mind, Jackie said, "I won't lie—it wasn't easy. Peace and acceptance didn't come for a long time. Some days I hurt more than others, but I didn't give up. My family, our pastor, and our friends wouldn't let me." She smiled at me, and her eyes glistened. "I wanted to run away or do something drastic. When I was right at the end of myself, my friend Sue told me, 'I'm praying for God to hold you so tightly you won't quit on life or on God.' That sounds simple, but just to know that Sue prayed for me every day—"

> God's peace seeped into my heart, and I was able to look at things differently.

"Like in the Bible when Aaron and Hur held up Moses's arms, she held up your arms when you couldn't hold them up yourself—"

"That's a nice way of saying it, and it's true." Jackie smiled before she added, "God's peace seeped into my heart, and I was able to look at things differently. I've been able to embrace a different dream for Joey."

In the three years I've known Jackie, I always felt serenity emanate from her. I assumed she had such a placid nature that nothing upset her. That day I met the victorious Jackie.

For perhaps twenty minutes she told me about her difficult adjustment. "God's grace was most important. But next to that, my friendship with other parents going through similar circumstances was the most helpful. They understood the heartache associated with caring for a seriously ill child. By sharing personal and practical resources with me, they taught me that it's possible for families to have a sense of normalcy."

That's when the first rays of hope entered my heart. *Jackie felt my pain.* Unable to speak again, I leaned forward and embraced her.

That day I finally understood that others had wept their way down the same path that led to tranquility and a quiet trust in a loving God. I found encouragement from Jackie, but most of all, through her I grasped God's presence with me.

God is with me.
God's friends are with me.
I am at peace.

Who Cares for Me?

Kelly's Story

She's the sick one. I'm often the invisible one, and I'm all right with that status. My mother is seriously ill. She needs to have people speak to her, touch her, and express concern.

But once in a while—especially when she's asleep and the lights are off—I lie in the dark and ask: *Who will take care of me? What if I get sick?* I try not to think those thoughts, but they come every now and then, sometimes more powerfully than others.

Occasionally the burden gets heavy, and I feel I can no longer carry my load. I memorized the Bible verse that says, "Give all your worries and cares to God, for he cares about you" (1 Peter 5:7).

I try to do exactly what the verse commands, but sometimes it's difficult.

As I finished praying that verse a few minutes ago, I laughed. God doesn't speak about what I might need then because I don't need to know that now. This much I know: God cares for my loved one in her sickness, and God also cares for me when I'm in need.

God cares for *me*.
That's enough to give me peace.

Expressions of Compassion

From Cec

"You can't *do* compassion; you *become* compassionate."

Where did those words come from? I don't know, but when I awakened Sunday morning, they repeatedly marched through my brain.

And I needed to listen to those words. I had focused on doing exactly the "right thing" for Shirley. Or, more accurately, I kept trying to figure out what the right thing was. The words inside my head forced me to ponder that as I drove alone to church while Shirley lay in bed at home.

I'm not a natural caregiver, at least not in the easygoing, faithful way some people seem to be. Our widowed daughter, C.C., is an example of that kind of person. She lives downstairs from us. Several times a day, she comes upstairs to help, and her actions seem effortless and natural.

I'm still learning what it means to be compassionate and give myself to Shirley and not to think about my work or my appointments. I haven't received a miraculous cure, but I'm slowly, slowly learning that it's more an act of the heart and a commitment than it is a physical action.

On Sunday, for instance, I spent most of the afternoon and evening in the chair next to the sofa where she lay. I got up to bring her ice water to take her medication with. I read the newspaper and an entire book during our quiet time together. Shirley also read most of the time. We didn't talk a great deal because perhaps there wasn't much to say.

It doesn't work like that every day, but I'm learning. I finally understood the words that had come to my mind that morning: "You can't *do* compassion; you *become* compassionate." My presence was my way of expressing my loving concern. I was at peace, and it was a restful time.

Shortly after I got into bed Sunday night, I thought about the day and realized I had become compassionate simply when I...

- cared for Shirley and *not* the things I needed to accomplish.
- sat there, next to her with no desire to be somewhere else.
- responded eagerly to her needs, whatever they were.
- demonstrated a willingness to stretch myself. (I'm not a cook, but I thawed and heated frozen food, and afterward cleaned up the kitchen.)

Compassion doesn't mean I have to do everything or provide for every need, but it does require a willingness to serve the person I love.

Until Death

From Cec and Twila

Most of us avoid using the word *death*. These days I hear people say, "When my mother passed…" Passing implies moving from one place to another. Death is a full stop at the end of the road. I feel as if they want to deny the reality and the finality of loss.

For those of us who are caregivers, we usually have time to think about the last stage of life. We see our loved one slowly creeping forward to the end of the road where that loved one will no longer be with us.

Even though we who are Christians have many biblical promises and assurances, at times we cringe and pull back. We don't know what death is like because we haven't experienced it.

We tend to see death only as a loss, an end to the way life used to be. For our loved ones, death may be a blessed relief after months or years of suffering and a fulfillment of their divine purpose on earth. They've gone ahead to wait for us. But for us death may mean the loss of our life companion and the grim notice that one day we too will follow. We see our loved one crossing the bridge and leaving us alone on this side. Regardless of how we view the end of this life, each of us must face the end by ourselves and in our own way.

We often experience a sense of loss and confusion. Grief fills our souls, and we don't know what to do next. For so long we've focused so much on lovingly caring for that one person that it feels as though we've taken a leave of absence from normal life.

> Like strangers in a new city, we often must begin again.

After the death of our loved one, we're forced back into life, and it may not be easy to return. People change; societal values haven't remained the same. Our church is filled with people we don't know. The friends we neglected during our time-out for caregiving have made new friends. Like strangers in a new city, we often must begin again.

We could come up with a seemingly endless list of adjustments we need to make, but they all come down to one thing: An important person—perhaps the most important person in our life—has died. We have to face the rest of life without that person.

Death has come between us, and even though we feel alone, God remains with us and reaches out to comfort us.

✖ ✖ ✖ ✖ ✖ ✖ ✖ ✖ ✖

We want to leave you with a few promises from the Bible as you face the reality of loss.

• Even when I walk through the darkest valley, I will not be afraid, for you are close beside me. Your rod and your staff protect and comfort me (Psalm 23:4).

• For God has said, "I will never fail you. I will never abandon you" (Hebrews 13:5).

• [Jesus said] Don't let your hearts be troubled. Trust in God, and trust also in me. There is more than enough room in my Father's home. If this were not so, would I have told you that I am going to prepare a place for you? (John 14:1-2).

• [Paul wrote] I am convinced that nothing can ever separate us from God's love. Neither death nor life, neither angels nor demons, neither our fears for today or our worries about tomorrow—not even the powers of hell can separate us from God's love (Romans 8:38).

Practical Suggestions...
God's Strength for Caregivers

- Don't let the person you love "turn into the disease." That is, remind yourself that the person is more important than the task.

- Listen, listen, listen to your loved one. Evaluate what he is saying or is trying to say before you act.

- Allow others to express compassion. Whether someone wants to bring in a meal, offers to clean your house, do your laundry, or sit with your loved one so you can get away for an hour or two, say yes.

- Don't cheat others out of opportunities to express their love. Ask God to help you be willing to accept any offer of friendship or practical help.

- Ask for help when you need it. Don't wait until you're exhausted or sick. *Ask now.* You don't have to be superwoman or superman; you only have to be human.

- In the beginning, do as little as you must for your loved one. Let your loved one have dignity and maintain control over parts of her life. She needs to hold on to as much independence as possible for as long as she can.

- Let the loved one indicate how much help he needs as long as it is safe and reasonable for him to do it alone. When it becomes unsafe or unreasonable, begin helping as gently as you can. Let your love embolden you to act for the other's good.

- When the situation demands that you get tough, do it. Whether it's with your loved one, medical issues, or legal matters, this is now your responsibility.

- Don't lose your sense of humor. Find ways to laugh. Read a humorous book or the comics, watch a TV sitcom, or rent a funny movie. A simple thing like that can lift your spirits and help you keep things in perspective.

> Don't let the person you love "turn into the disease."

- Forgive yourself for not being perfect. You will fail at times. It's as simple as saying, "God, forgive me and help me forgive myself for..."

- Get out of the house whenever you can, even if it's only for minutes at a time. Read a paper or a book; sit on the porch; join the local Y or health spa. You might go for a walk and enjoy the breeze and the warm sunshine on your face. As you walk, remind yourself that your legs are able to carry you wherever you want to go and thank God for that ability.

- Take notes or keep a journal, especially if you administer meds or physical therapy of any kind. It's easier to check a journal than to keep the information in your memory during stressful situations.

- Educate yourself. The more you know about what you're dealing with, the more you will feel confident and in control when you must make difficult decisions, and the less often you'll have to second-guess what needs to be done.

- The Internet is an excellent source of information about the disease and for caregiving. Many sites cater specifically to caregivers. Some are divided by the diagnosis, such as dementia, cancer, or Parkinson's.

- Someone was quoted as saying, "And it came to pass" in reference to facing difficult times. "The situation didn't come to stay," she said. Remind yourself that some days are more stressful than others. Relish the good days.

- Pray each day. Spending time with God will remind you that God cares and will strengthen you in your weakest moments.

Practical Suggestions…Because You Can No Longer Cope

- One day you may have to say, "Dear God, I can't go on. She needs more than I can give." Remind yourself that this isn't the end, but only the next step in your long-term caregiving.

- Remind yourself that you have not failed. You have succeeded in expressing love, commitment, and compassion to the seriously ill person you love.

- Get professional help for yourself. Talk to your pastor or spiritual advisor. Ask the medical staff. Investigate the options open to you.

- Ask your friends to pray for you so that you can move ahead and do what's best for your loved one. This isn't merely a decision about you. This is a decision about the good of your loved one.